The Dig Deep Method

Finding Truth in Information.
Applying Critical Thinking
To
Veterinary Medical Aromatherapy®
And Other Possibilities

Dr. Nancy Brandt,
the Pioneering Veterinarian in Veterinary Medical Aromatherapy®

Copyright © 2018 by Spark Education LLC.

All rights reserved. No part of this publication may be reproduced, distributed, or transmitted in any form or by any means, including photocopying, recording, or other electronic or mechanical methods, without the prior written permission of the publisher, except in the case of brief quotations embodied in critical reviews and certain other noncommercial uses permitted by copyright law.

Ordering Information
www.safe4animals.com

Printed in the United States of America

Disclaimer

The information presented herein is in no way intended to treat, cure, diagnose or prevent any disease or illness. If you feel that you have a medical condition you are urged to seek the help of a medical professional. You are encouraged to first seek the counsel of your health care professional before making any changes to your current health routine. The suggestions in this book are for use with Biologically Active® essential oils as appropriately labeled for use. This book is being distributed with the understanding the publisher and the authors are not liable for the misconception or misuse of the information provided.

Table of Contents:

Dedication

About the Author

Introduction

PART I: Dig Deep Method

    Step 1: Do you have the full story?

    Step 2: What specifically was used?

    Step 3: What techniques were employed?

    Step 4: What treatments and diagnostics were used?

    Step 5: Was there a true correlation drawn? How did they prove X caused Y?

    Step 6: What experts were consulted? Are they qualified?

    Step 7: Are there any references used to back up what they believe?

    Step 8: Did you Dig Deep into the actual studies or references cited?

    Step 9: Is the study valid that was used to substantiate their claim?

    Step 10: RELAX – Dig Deep – Educate – Yourself – Use Precision

PART II: A Story of Perspective

PART III: The Precision Model

PART IV: Making Sense of Research Papers

PART V: cGMP/QC - Picking Partners

Dedication

To my adoptive family:

Jim and Marcella Vonn Harting
Dallas Harting
Luke and Kortni Langsweirdt
Grandma Kay and Grandpa Cal

Thank you for adopting me and my family into yours and asking quality questions that lead to this book, among many other gifts. My life is enriched knowing all of you and sharing our desire to educate those who listen to the amazing world of essential oils.

About the Author:

When someone asks me, "What do you do?" I reply, "How much time do you have?" What a person does often requires many hats.

I am an integrative veterinarian, a Mother and Grandmother, a friend and animal lover.

I am a network marketer reaching the top 0.1% of the company's rank.

I am the pioneering veterinarian for Veterinary Medical Aromatherapy® (VMA) and the safe and effective use of aromatherapy in animals.

I am a keynote speaker, author and published writer.

I am a researcher, investigator, treasure hunter and problem solver.

I am the CEO of three companies.

I am the Founder of Veterinary Medical Aromatherapy Association and designed and teach the only RACE approved VMA® course to certify animal caregivers.

I am a Professor for an Oriental Medical School.

I am an intuitive healer and Seraphim Blueprint Teacher.

I am a Life Coach Facilitator and counselor.

I am an avid learner, especially of Quantum Biology and Human Behavior.

I am a Spirit having an Earthly Journey.

The list can continue. These are the hats that I wear. Under them all I am an inquisitive woman that believes there is
"Truth in all things and nothing is THE TRUTH"

I believe that anything is possible – Anything!!
If we can dream it we can do it. Our time, intention, money and attention is the exchange necessary to bring dreams to fruition. I believe that information is just someone's opinion and by diving into their ideas one may emerge with a greater understanding of what we, ourselves, believe.

The Journey on this planet is to collect experiences and combine them with our own uniqueness to develop and evolve as a spirit having a human adventure. My choice for you is to read this book and discover a method of investigation into your experience of this Earthly journey and discover what is Truth for you.

Introduction:

Why Look into Digging Deep?

Are you the personality type that excitedly jumps right in to a new possibility, opportunity or project?
Or
Are you the personality type that jumps in after careful deliberation of all the facts?

If you jump right in you may expect everyone to jump right in. If you research and need all the facts, the person who jumps right in may overwhelm you with excitement.
Or
You, the researcher, may give a person who jumps right in way too much detail.

Which one are you?

The Dig Deep Method supports any level of fact finding. Ultimately, we really want to trust our facts that support the use of essential oils in pets, Veterinary Medical Aromatherapy®. The Dig Deep Method can really apply to any opportunity. Dig Deep digs through the information overload and marketing ploys to find the hidden treasure of the truth.

The Dig Deep Method can be applied to any investigation you are excited to incorporate into your life.

1. Where would you find your information or facts?
2. How would you know if those facts are substantiated or true?
3. Is social media true or false? Have you ever read a headline of a post and ran with the headline as if it were true?
4. Have you ever watched a newscast and believed every word, getting up in arms to march against a cause?

The Dig Deep Method is a way to apply a step-by-step analysis to unearth any truth in the story.

Quality matters especially when it comes to pets. Quality, specifically applies to information one may use to substantiate or ban the use of essential oils. In today's internet of finding everything at our fingertips, how can we dig deep into the information overload and become treasure hunters of truth?

We must find gems of truth amongst all the information for profit marketing?

With the Dig Deep Method you really are digging for hidden treasure in the Search Engine Optimized Internet world.

How many of you stop at the first page of a Google search? How many of you read the headline on a social media post and extrapolate a meaning from just that surface detail?

How deep are you willing to dig for truth?

I choose to take you on a journey toward becoming a critical thinker and asking the question "Does this make sense?"

Choose to no longer be mislead into a rabbit hole of sensationalized for profit news headlines ever again.

Use the 10 steps in the Dig Deep Method to increase and enhance, even more, the power of your common sense and critical thinking. Break free of the blinders to see the truth.

Stop hitting your head against the wall of misinformation.

A. You can apply this Dig Deep Method to many aspects of your life. Ask the question do I have enough information to make an informed decision about what I was just told, read, heard etc.? This booklet is about how I apply critical thinking to the selection and use of essential oils in pets. This is my method of hunting for treasure.

B. I will give you a model to use to Dig Deep into why people use excuses and lack perspective and insight into what would help them the most.

C. I will also give you ways of Digging Deep into research and sorting out its validity. How do you know if the research is skewed in favor of an outcome? How do you know if the cited research applies to the problem at hand?

D. Finally I will give you quality questions to ask in regards to cGMP/QC, that is current Good Manufacturing Processes and Quality Control. How do you Dig Deep into the companies you choose to purchase from or do business with?

How many times have you been lead to believe "??????" only to find out it was not true at all? Let's take the blinders off!!

The Dig Deep Method

Note Page

PART I: Dig Deep Method

The 10 steps in the Dig Deep Method

- [ ] **Step 1:** Do you have the full story?

- [ ] **Step 2:** What specifically was used?

- [ ] **Step 3:** What techniques were employed?

- [ ] **Step 4:** What treatments and diagnostics were used?

- [ ] **Step 5:** Was there a true correlation drawn? How did they prove X caused Y?

- [ ] **Step 6:** What experts were consulted? Are they qualified?

- [ ] **Step 7:** Are there any references used to back up what they believe?

- [ ] **Step 8:** Did you Dig Deep into the actual studies or references cited?

- [ ] **Step 9:** Is the study valid that was used to substantiate their claim?

- [ ] **Step 10:** RELAX – Dig Deep – Educate Yourself – Use Precision

The details of the 10 steps of the Dig Deep Method with detail.

Step 1: Do you have the full story? Do you understand the details? Are you educated and have experience with what is being said? Are they speaking your language?

For Example – stock reporting for me is like someone speaking French and I need a translator who speaks "stocks."

For other folks, confusion may result by watching "Grey's Anatomy" with all the medical language becoming just back ground noise gibberish - until we get to the really McDreamy juicy parts?

As a medical professional, for me, the medicine can be educational at times and other times it is simply just WRONG. I speak medicine. ☺

Step 1 can be the game changer. This can be the question that throws that news article or blog post in the recycle pile.

The closer you are to the full story the better the picture of what really happened.

I call this part collecting puzzle pieces. A puzzle will reveal a picture or a story. Without all the pieces we often draw a conclusion that is untrue.

Sensational headlines draw the reader in. Fear tactics keep us reading.

And of course reading leads to more hits and ratings - which lead to more sponsorship. So many will monetize your terror. So many withhold revealing puzzle pieces.

Are you being duped into reading a very skewed view? Are you taking valuable energy and emotion and being lead down a rabbit hole to see only one piece of the puzzle?

Just ask, "Do I have the full unbiased story? " Is this the truth? Do I have enough puzzle pieces of information to see the real picture?

Step 2: What essential oils specifically were used?

A. Did they use cheap imitations or Biologically Active® essential oils? You must scrutinize the materials used in this story or study. This is a buyer beware world.

I was told this story by a man who has traveled worldwide in his field:

He discovered some herbal products for export were found to be composed of brick dust. I asked him how he knew this, and he said he saw it with his own eyes. He had photos. He witnessed workers breaking down used bricks with hammers to dust, and then put the dust into capsules to be labeled and sold as supplements. I asked how do they get away with this? He said they bury these so the samples they take for quality control are on the top[1].

Can you imagine the profits made? Can you imagine how you would feel if you found out your calcium product was just brick dust? What would you look for to make sure this does not happen to you.

B. Is the Botanical name clear:
    Lavender vs *Lavendula angustifolia*

C. Is there a batch number present for the distillation?
D. In which region was the plant grown?
    Helichrysum grown in Washington State rather than Croatia will not be the same plant or yield the same oil.
E. What method of distillation was used?
F. What are the standards of current Good Manufacturing practices and quality control that are in place?
G. What tests were performed to assure the oils are natural and not synthetic?

Find your trusted supplier dedicated to the highest standards for Good Manufacturing Practices (cGMP) and Quality Control (QC).

Most research studies are conducted on synthetic essential oils because they have a consistency of chemistry - whereas natural plants can vary with different environmental conditions.

Biologically Active® essential oils will vary in color, consistency and even aromas.

This is why asking about testing and the TYPE of essential oil used is vital so we can compare the same items across research articles or incidence reports.

If we are saying lavender killed my cat, it means nothing until we can dig deep enough to realize lavender was not the only thing in the bottle.

It may have been laden with adulterants - such as hexane.

It was likely not even *Lavendula angustifolia,* but in fact was Lavindin *(Lavandula x intermedia)*, which is high in camphor.

An entirely different chemistry leads to an entirely different set of reactions. How would you feel if research on a blood pressure medication was found to use an entirely different pharmaceutical? Would you continue to believe the study? Would you even trust the medicine?

Step 3: What techniques were employed?

What methods were used for application of the essential oil?

In some studies, upwards of 5 – 15 mls of undiluted essential oil was given to rats via ingestion before any reported side effects[2].

In research, we have to eliminate as many variables as possible. Sometimes the researcher does not realize they purchased an adulterated essential oil or had unforeseen "tag alongs" they did not adjust for.

Impurities in the air, in the diluents used or on the skin of the animal will combine with essential oils and cause an entirely different chemical reaction. Just like combining certain pharmaceuticals can be fatal.

Have they noted all the variables? Have they noted the techniques used? Have they investigated their techniques for any unforeseen variables? (Tag alongs)

Which water has "tag alongs?"

-VS-

The Questions to ask are:

How much oil was used?

How frequent were the oils dosed - every day and for how long?

Was the application neat or diluted?

What diluent was used and was it pure?

Were there any other "tag alongs" or impurities that may have accounted for the unforeseen reactions?

Did they, in fact, control all the variables?

Did they really use a Biologically Active® essential oil?

I have offered mini-private lectures for 20 years now in Veterinary Medical Aromatherapy® (VMA)[3]. I, therefore, have had opportunities to hear many stories of essential oil use above and beyond those in my clinical studies.

Many years ago I had a lady contact me for answers about her birds.

She had been diffusing oils for five days in Buffalo, NY during winter, and called me to find out what happened to cause her birds to die - yes I said died!

**I had to dig deep collecting puzzle
pieces to get some answers**

What I found was this:

1. She had diffused for five days straight - no break.

2. The diffuser type used, was the atomizing type so the oil was not diluted with water like ultrasonic types do.

3. She had used 105 mls of a proprietary essential oil blend that is highly anti-microbial and in the aromatherapy world, is used with less frequency and concentration, normally. It was, however, a highly Biologically Active® essential oil and very pure.

4. Her home was 750 square feet, and sealed up for the cold Buffalo, NY winter.

5. Her home was very dirty with dust and mold. That is why she was diffusing so much.

6. She would leave often during the diffusing to run errands, and as she said "get a breath of fresh air".

Her first bird died on the fifth night. She lost four birds varying in age from 5 to 56. It was truly tragic to lose her four closest family members. My heart reached out to hug this grieving mother.

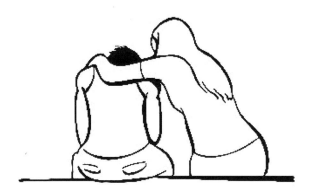

One necropsy was performed at my request. The birds' lungs were full of a black tar. The vet felt the essential oils were the cause. Upon analysis and research for this case, I learned about impurities in the air being gobbled up by the essential oils and then dropping onto surfaces thus purifying the air. This complex may be inhaled and can cause issues in small animals, especially birds.

In the case of the birds, this residue manifested as the tar in their lungs

Remember birds are small, they have a sensitive respiratory system and they had no way to move away from the soot resulting from the combination of many misguided techniques used here.

Just like the

**canary in the coal mine –
the birds suffered from poor technique**

What are the logical questions to ask? Did they use inhalation, ingestion or topical applications? What else could it be? Was there an escape route from the diffusing essential oils?

Often the cause of the side effect is the technique used, not the essential oil.

An example of similar "technique cause" is similar to being given a drug and told to take 1 pill every 12 hours for 3 weeks. That is a total of 42 pills. Instead, you use a different technique and think it is quicker to ingest the whole bottle at once; you overdose, get very sick or die.

When poor technique meets poor quality essential oils, we now have too many variables to blame the essential oils. To label the oil 100% pure, all they have to do is put 1% pure oil in the bottle. Please be alert and aware, educate yourself and consult a trained veterinarian in VMA® (Veterinary Medical Aromatherapy®). VMAA.vet.

Step 4: What treatments and diagnostics were used for the reported symptoms?

What were the treatments and diagnostics used? Who did the treatments and diagnostics used for the reported symptoms, illness or death? The birds necropsy was very telling, especially analysis of the tarry substance showing NO components of the essential oil blend.

Ask - How did they prove it was indeed the essential oils as the only cause?

Cause and effect or "if this then that" – is not always a correlated truth

If I walk out into the sunshine and a stray bullet hits me, was it the sunshine that killed me? Was it walking into the sunshine that killed me or was it a stray bullet? If you knew nothing of gunshots, bullets, or did not know to look for wounds, you may conclude the sun caused my death because that was the last thing I was doing. Make Sense?

Let's look at it like this - If you eat a lot of fatty foods and you die of a heart attack it must have been the fatty foods right? What if this person also drank a lot of water, could the water be at cause? Why would we choose the fatty foods? We chose the fatty foods because they've been researched and found a correlation in 100's of studies that fatty foods increase the chance of heart attacks.

100's of correlations vs just one
Incident leads to better conclusions

If I drink water and then I sneeze, was the water at cause? How would I know? Simple -- drink water with no variables (doing nothing else) repeatedly and measure how many times you sneeze. Analyze the data to see if there is a statistically relevant correlation. In most people, water will not cause them to sneeze, so likely the two are not related.

There was another cause of the sneeze.

A variable unaccounted for.

The puzzle piece left out of this story was that I had just bit into a cracker with a lot of pepper and I was taking a drink of water to wash it down.

Now what may be more likely the cause for the sneeze? The pepper – of course! Or do we need to run many courses of eating the cracker then drinking the water to see if it was the combo of the two or just the cracker with pepper. That is research method refined.

With essential oil related stories or articles:
Ask what were the symptoms of the intoxication?
Was the veterinarian educated on essential oil toxicity?
Without evidence of a correlation, we jump to believing "drinking water causes sneezing" – but without enough information.

Like in the bird story, the black tar had NO essential oil components in it; it was mold spores.

VMAA.vet is doing constant outreach to educate the public and animal caregivers who want to get to the truth.
How I diffuse for all animals and especially birds changed a lot after this bird incident. Their lives have served a higher purpose.

I develop my protocols to be both safe and effective. More controlled studies are needed, more analysis of previous claims are needed.

In Robert Tisserand's and Rodney Young's book "Essential Oil Safety" they cite hundreds of studies that substantiate the safety of essential oils and found many studies to be misguided and false.

Robert Tisserand states in his book, studies are: key to

"help minimize any risk of harm associated with the use of (essential) oils, while optimizing their beneficial effects... rational assessments of risk by critically evaluating and extrapolating from available information relating to both the effects of essential oils and of their individual constituents, from in vivo and in vitro human and animal studies. We have read many excellent reports, as well as some seriously misguided ones. "

"Much of the safety information available online is misleading, confusing, wrong or simply absent."

"The quality of essential oils is an important issue for anyone using them therapeutically. Confidence in their safe use begins with ensuring that the oils have a known botanical origin and composition."

"Many biological studies have been reported using essential oils whose composition has not been clearly stated or even determined."

"In some studies, observations were made only after administering extremely high doses."[4]

Essential oil safety is covered in more detail in the VMA® course. www.safe4animals.com

Step 5: Was there a true correlation drawn? How did they prove it was the Essential oil that was at cause?

This really follows up on step 4's data collection and is asking the question what was used to support their hypothesis that the essential oils were the cause of the effect (ie) symptoms, illness, or death.

Did they rush to a conclusion?

Were the oils the primary cause?

Were the oils a contributory cause – like in the birds?
Or were the essential oils part of an unsubstantiated cause and effect claim? Like the water causing sneezing.

Many incident reporting databases are unsubstantiated claims

Case study after case study in my practice only leads to the need to do further research. Clinical studies and double blinded studies are needed. Using exquisite scientific method - eliminating variables and drawing true conclusions of safe and effective Veterinary Medical Aromatherapy® is vital.

Dr Pierre Franchomme, at our last shared speaking engagement, spoke of research on the batch number of an essential oil. Some reported effects are tied to a very specific batch of oils only. Not every batch yields the same effects[5].

Just another reason to trust who you purchase essential oils from.

We have to look for double standards like:

All oils are bad because of one incident
or
This oil will cure it all based on one testimonial

We have to develop evidence-based standards of safe and effective use of VMA® in animals. Is the research valid that is used in backing up our claims or is there a bias?

VMAA.vet endeavors to do this treasure hunting methodically-

Money and ethics are the limiting factors at this time.
Money is needed to finance the studies.
Animals becoming imprisoned to do the research - is my moral ethical limitation.

I was asked to do a study in cats to find the LD_{50} of tea tree oil. The LD_{50} stands for the lethal dose 50% of the time or 50% of pets die. To design this study, I would have to adopt 80 cats from the shelter with similar physiological traits as possible. Then dose them with *Melaleuca alternifolia* enough to kill 50% of the cats and possibly harming the others. Then perform a necropsy in all 80 cats - yes kill them all – and then prove the essential oil was the only causal agent in the deaths. I then could report the amount of essential oil needed to kill cats 50% of the time.

I could not be a part of this type of research.
This is not my path.

This is the development of evidence-based standards of safe and effective medical use. This is easy to do in pharmacological research studies that are currently the recognized standard research models.

Many, many animals are sacrificed for this work. Surely, we can find a better way?

I did not take part in this project, instead I found some references to essential oil LD_{50}'s in children and extrapolated that data to use for cats.

The aching question in my heart is - did 50% of children have to die to find the LD_{50} or was this data extrapolated from rat experiments? What do you think the answer is?

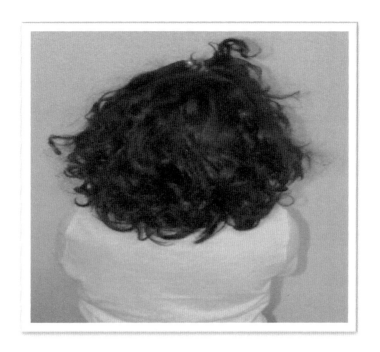

Step 6: What experts were consulted? Are they qualified?

Who are the experts that were consulted? What affiliations might they be speaking for? Do they own stock in the company doing the research? My research has been independent of affiliations, as I have used many company's oils. I do have my recommendations after 20 years in the industry. Were the experts even named?
    Sometimes the article will just say "experts said….. "

What qualifications do they have to speak to this specialized field of VMA®?

Were they involved in the case or called in as an outside expert? Many times the experts never even saw the case or looked over any of the puzzle pieces. They are really giving you their opinion. Sometimes that opinion is not even aware of the puzzle pieces at all.

Veterinary Medical Aromatherapy® is not routinely taught. Currently, the Veterinary Medical Aromatherapy Association has the only R.A.C.E. approved course for training VMA®. VMAA.vet

Many times opinion, beliefs, speculation and bias are presented as education and true information.

What is the true intent of this story, article or news segment? Is this mis-information or mis-education? Has this been sensationalized for ratings sake?

> **BECOME TRUTH SEEKERS - NOT OPINION COLLECTORS**

7: Are there any references used to back up what they believe?

Do not take on a belief without Digging Deeper. Find the real treasure - do not settle for less.
Who educated the writer or speaker? Who educated their educators? Did they include references? Can you find the references? Will they share their data?

Research papers were developed as a way to share data and findings in an effort to further other research.
They were NEVER – I repeat NEVER – intended to be proof of efficacy or safety like they are now being used in Evidence – Based Medicine.

> **It is time to fix the system of proof and truth**

What data influenced "the expert" to have this belief?
One case or many cases???

In good scientific method, we eliminate "observer biases" as much as possible, yet bias is inherent just in formulating a belief (the expert for instance has bias).

Let's look at bias and the observer principle of quantum mechanics through this example:

Look around your surroundings right now and do only my first instructions. Stay on this page.
Find and count all the RED objects in your line of sight.

All the RED
Just RED
Add up all the RED
RED
RED
RED

STOP READING HERE AND FIND RED – RED – RED

The Dig Deep Method

Note Page

Now - look at this book and while keeping your eyes on the book only remember how much GREEN there was in your sight line. EYES DOWN!!!

No - keep your eyes fixed on this book. How much GREEN was in your sight line? EYES DOWN!!!!!

How many of you only noticed RED in this exercise? Be truthful!

Why did we see red and not notice green in this exercise?

Because I gave you a bias in the beginning of looking for RED.

This means the Observer – you – activated your RAS – or Reticulating Activating System – within your brainstem to filter for RED only.

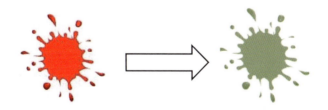

This is survival level hard wiring in the brain designed to look for <u>the bias</u> - or the danger.

When we set a hypothesis - we set a bias right from the beginning.

If you believe the treatment will work
you are right.
If you believe the treatment will NOT work
you are also right.

Whatever you believe to be true is what your RAS will search for in the research data or see in the puzzle pieces. This is why Double Blind studies hold more weight or validity.

Bias still occurs in Double Blind Studies, by how the study is designed, like the bias of thinking the quality of the essential oil does not matter and we know they are not all created equal.

It is always a matter of perspective. Seeing an outcome – deciding what to blame – or coming to conclusions about the data may be fraught with bias. Humans are meaning making machines.

If you are looking for Pugs in this puzzle - when the pieces come together to form a Pug - you stop and formulate a conclusion that the puzzle is all about Pugs. You basically do not see anything except Pugs. The rest is like white out.

Just like when you looked for red, you did not notice the rest of the data, all the other colors, in your sight line.
This is bias.

In the case of this puzzle pictured, you would have missed the rest of the data or picture and drawn the wrong conclusion that the picture was all about Pugs. Here we take off the bias blinders and reveal the puzzle was much more than a Pug.

The observer principle of Quantum Physics proves bias skews the research in favor of the hypothesis. Of course this is only a belief and hypothesis. ☺ However, a highly substantiated one.

Step 8: Did you Dig Deep into the actual studies cited?

The regulatory organizations, like the FDA, demand scientific proof before we can make claims of safety or efficacy.

Ask if the study is scientifically verifiable?
What scientific method was applied to the study?
Learn how to dig into research and pull out valid treasures.
Don't allow a double standard to exist

$$1 \text{ case} = \text{BAD}$$
$$\text{or}$$
$$1 \text{ case} = \text{GOOD}$$

There is more on this step in Part IV.

Step 9: What type of study was used to substantiate their claim?

Incident reports and/or Meta-studies may or may not have been verified for the same variables when it comes to essential oils. The researcher may not know what to look for – like RED vs GREEN.

Most studies in regards to essential oils, are comparing Apples to Oranges and grouping them together in one meta study or incident report. This frequently happens and skews the reporting conclusions.

Not all essential oils and techniques and research studies are created equally, therefore the grouped studies, like poison control incident reports or even meta-studies for evaluating many research papers, may not validate or invalidate essential oil use.

They may _not_ have taken into account all the variables inherent in essential oil research.

It would be like postulating ALL antibiotics are bad because many people vomit after taking antibiotics.

This is NOT true for ALL antibiotics. Instead, each individual antibiotic should be studied and reported on its own merit. Some antibiotics are safer than others and some are more likely to cause side effects like vomiting.

We would have to break each of those individual antibiotic studies down into the different age brackets or physiologic condition of the individuals taking them; for instance, microbiome health. And so on and so forth until we are comparing apples to apples and accounting for all the variables.

The more specific we are the more truth is unearthed.

**Avoid
ALL or
NONE
Statements**

Step 10: RELAX – Dig Deep – Educate Yourself – Use Precision

Become a critical thinker

Gain Perspective

Learn to use the Precision Model

Learn to understand research and glean its hidden treasures

Understand, cGMP and QC

Remember to let your pet participate in its own rescue.
Learn how to select oils safely and effectively.

Educate yourself:

Go to Safe4animals.com
1. To find many free videos.
2. My books
3. The VMA® courses

Go to VMAA.vet
1. To find a trained animal caregiver.
2. To join the cause and organization setting the standards for safe and effective use of VMA®.

The most important question to Ask is –
Is this True and what else could this be or mean?

PART II: A Story of Perspective

A beautiful little girl, Daisy, around 4 or 5 years of age, looked up into the wizen eyes of her Grandfather and asked:

"Why are all those flies hitting against that little window above the cows getting milked?"

Grandpa said, "That is what they do. Hundreds and hundreds just follow each other into the window. Knocking their heads against the glass, over and over again. They are believing that is the way outside to many great choices. Many of them die without ever doing much of anything else my little darling girl."

Beautiful blue eyes looked up at all those flies, dying in that little window, and tears welled up in her eyes. She asked, "Grandpa can't they see another way? Do they want to be trapped in this one way of doing things?"

This long time dairy farmer just smiled at his inquisitive smart little helper and said, "Well if that is how they see things, who am I to say differently?"

She looked at the large pile of dead flies. She thought long and hard and then finally exclaimed, "Grandpa there is another way!!!! They don't all have to believe this is the only way to get outside to all their dreams."

The Farmer recognized in her the passion to help those flies. He saw how much their pain, of hitting their heads against the wall, hurt this little precious soul.

With excitement, he asked her for her new perspective, "What do you know that I don't know sweetheart?"

She said enthusiastically, "Grandpa those big barn doors just over there are always open – big – wide and no window – they could fly over there and be free outside to find all their dreams!" and then with a little despondency she said shaking her head, "Grandpa how do we convince them that door is a better choice? How can I help them discover their freedom is just behind them?"

He said, "I guess, little one, you will have to use precision to direct one fly at a time to the barn door and maybe many will adopt this new belief or perspective and fly without restraint."

She hurried to get a broom and began the joy of moving the fly's choice from "death by window" to "full freedom by wide open door". All day she worked hard reeducating these flies and re-designing their methods.

Some listened and found freedom. Others would not change their mind no matter what she did; they just kept banging their heads against the window hoping to get a different result until they died.

Grandpa and beautiful Daisy went down to the house, hand-in-hand, for dinner, satisfied they had spent the day helping others find new possibilities.

PART III: The Precision Model

A Bit on the Precision Model:

Richard Bandler and John Grinder, as a way to add new resources and references to limiting perceptions or situations (red vs green), developed the Precision Model.

The Precision Model leads to digging deeper and can cause someone to reevaluate his or her bias. This is especially helpful when speaking with individuals you know will be assisted by essential oils or other integrative medical choices and they are sticking to one focus or bias minded. Like Daisy, you could help them find a better way they did not know is even there for them.

Using the Precision Model

According to Tony Robbins, a results coach and speaker, the purpose of the Precision Model is to add new resources and new references to a limiting perception or situation[6]. This creates new possibilities.

Richard Bandler and John Grinder developed this "meta model" as a tool that can cause someone to reevaluate what is actually occurring that causes them to create meaning in their world.

What do you see here:

And here:

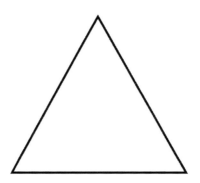

The Dig Deep Method

Note Page

Now what do you see:

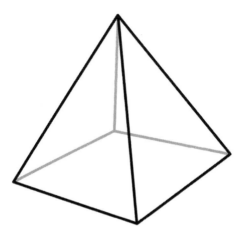

Which one is the correct perspective?

Using Precision is helping people see different perspectives by going on a treasure hunt for how they arrived at their current meaning and allowing them to come up with a better plan of action.

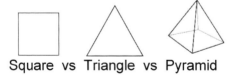

> **Asking them quality questions can produce an even more empowering meaning or belief**

In simple terms, just get curious to do precision. When I use this technique I'm truly curious as to how they came to the thinking, meaning or language they are choosing to use.

If I am seeing a "pyramid" and they keep speaking of a "square", I use precision questions to see their perspective and then help them see mine.

The very first and most important question I ask is:

> Is this True?
> *For the flies, is the window the best choice*

Next I align with what they believe is true and ask for specificity.

> I'm curious, could you explain how this (the statement) is true?
> *Why are the flies bashing into the window?*

Next I ask:

> What would happen if this (statement) were not true?
> Can you think of a time when this was not true?
> What else could this be?

If the window is not the way out, is it possible there is another way? Did any fly ever get outside by any other means?

> **People will come up with their own solutions or their own new possibility.**

My outcome of using the precision model is to hunt down the treasures of choices within themselves (things they already know) that assist them (the observer) in finding a more resourceful meaning, choice or truth. We often know a better way; we just are so focused on the current way of doing things.

We are so focused on RED, we find red therefore missing the green. As soon as we remember to notice GREEN, we see it.

When language is fluffy it can be difficult to take effective action because you have not dug deep into understanding the real issue. The language is not specific.

"All essential oils are bad for cats?"

If we dig in with precision, we can understand where they got their fear, and help them understand other possibilities.

1. Generalizing gets in the way of effective action.

2. Precision improves effective collaboration.

3. Precision helps reduce ambiguity and leads to a clear picture of that hidden treasure of what they really want, need or desire.

4. Use precision in your own communication and use precision with others by getting curious about what and why they believe the way they do.

5. Stop banging against the window, like the flies, expecting a different result.

You can help a person:

1. Trapped in pain to find the light at the end of the tunnel.

2. Access rich resources within themselves they had buried away.

3. Help them acknowledge their true desires and needs and make better choices.

4. Find the patterns of thinking that are preventing them from getting what they desire in life.

5. Access leverage for them to want to change and improve or go after what they say they want.

6. Make it their idea and not yours.

No one wants to be told to or sold to. They want to feel great about their own discovery of how to help themselves and others. They want to feel empowered with perspective on the choices they chose to make or take.

Swishing the flies with a broom just got them to turn on a new flight path and then they made the choice to fly out of the barn doors to bigger and better adventures. We did not build barn doors, they were always there. We helped the flies discover a better way.

Use your hands to remember the keys to Precision

Finger	Right hand ⬇ Lacks perspective	Left hand ⬇ Resourceful
Pinky	universals	all, every, never
Ring	mind reading	what will??
Middle	verbs	how specifically
Pointer	Nouns	who or what
Thumb	TOO ….	Compared to

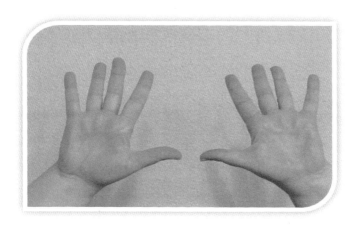

Merging the right and left hands gives you the shovel to dig deep for the treasure of what they really mean, want or choose to have. Clear concise language will lead you to a clear concise picture of the need or desire, they are really meaning to have met. Listen for the non-perspective, non-concise words to give you the better questions to ask.

Like the broom directed the flies to see a better way.

    1. "The experts say that essential oils are dangerous."

      ? Which experts? Which article is that in? How did the article come to that conclusion?

    2. "Well really - I'm scared I'll hurt my pet."

      (Ah, we are closer to the real reason.)

      ? What about the oils causes you to have fear?

Can you think of a time when you had this fear and acted anyway? Why do you think you acted then?

This allows them to see how they take action in spite of fear.

= **Listen for Universals** – Right Pinky

All people need oxygen vs All people need pure oxygen. Limited truth to generalized truth or usually true.

1. "This article said essential oils harmed a cat. Therefore, I now believe all oils harm cats". Limited truth of limited study of <u>one</u> cat became generalized belief of all cats.

 = Ask – Left Pinky

Are there articles in which essential oils do not harm cats? Is this true all the time? Really never ever or what else could this mean? Can you remember a time when this was not true? Does one equal all?

 = **Listen for Mind Reading** – Right Ring

Should, shouldn't, must, can't

These are generalizations that get in the way of effective action. They can limit and paralyze action and perspective. This is like putting blinders on or running down a rabbit hole chasing down a possibility only to now not be able to see any other perspective. (Like RED and not seeing GREEN).

1. "Only a western trained vet has all the answers."

This deletes all integrative veterinarians who have significantly more years and areas of study as a possibility.

2. "I can't do that. "

What would happen now that you have?

? = Ask – Left Ring

What would happen if you...?
What prevents you from...?
What causes you to...?
Have you considered.....?

= **Listen for Verbs** – Right Middle

"I feel very scared. "

Getting more information about what is at the cause of the feeling can shed light on the solution. These are poorly actionable statements. This is where I get curious to find the treasure or incident that created this generalization.

 = Ask – Left Middle

When you need clarity on what actions lead to the end state.
Can you remember a time when you were not scared?
What did you do then?
How specifically does "scared" happen?
What do you do that causes "scared" to occur?
How do you know when "scared" will occur?

 = **Listen for Nouns** – Right Pointer

Fluffy language is unspecific language like people, they, the experts, etc.

1. "They never understand me." Who specifically?
2. "The experts say." Which experts? What qualifies them as experts?

❓ = Ask – Left Pointer

When you are not sure who or what is performing the action.

Who or what specifically?

Who does not understand you?

What is the thing that creates this belief?

 = **Listen for TOO …. Excuse** – Right Thumb

Too much, too many, too expensive etc.

These are ways to delete without evidence.

These are the fluffy excuse on top of other excuses and finally covering the real one. – Fear of change

1. "This essential oil is too expensive!"
   Compared to what? A $45,000 trip to the ER?

❓ = Ask – Left Thumb

Use this when you do not know the basis of comparison.

Too much. Compared to what?

Too many. Compared to what?

Too expensive. Compared to what?

Too saturated. Compared to what?

> Remember to make what "they think is right" into what else "they now know to be possible"

PART IV: Reading Research Papers

Some steps to better understanding research papers:

Should you believe the research findings?
Do they apply to what you are using them for?
Are Truth and Right the same thing?

Go back and remEmber:

Square vs Triangle vs Pyramid

Who was right?

Square?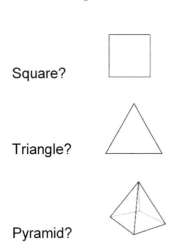

Triangle?

Pyramid?

Whatever you saw was right. If you saw the square and were not given other data then the conclusion is the object is a square we are looking at.

If you saw the triangle, the outcome is similar.

If you saw the pyramid you would have collected more data and of course come to a different conclusion.

> **All perspectives are right and supported by data but only one is true**

Research papers were intended as a way for researchers to share and communicate their findings. They wanted a way to open dialogs with colleagues about their observations. They then could collect more data points and build better research plans they could collaborate even better on, finding the truth.

For instance, if the person looking at a square shared their data with the person looking at the triangle, they may build a better research model and discover they were both looking at different aspects of a pyramid.

Research was NEVER intended as proof of anything only another piece of the puzzle building toward the truth.

Research can be messy.
Research often disagrees.
It is important to distinguish strong results from weak ones.

> **Research is flawed and I'll prove it with research!!**

The Research Paper is divided into subheadings:

1. Abstract   Do I care about the study?
2. Tables   What did they really find?
3. Methods   Do I believe the results of the table?
4. Discussion   So what do the results mean?
5. Lit. Review   What did we already know?
6. Peer Review   Do the peers believe the study?

When reading a paper, look to identify each section. Look up definitions of any terms which you do not understand. Identify the purpose of the paper. This step is really key to many drug test papers. If the purpose is to support a company viewpoint, the paper may have design flaws because they are really "only looking for RED".

Gain an understanding of the methods. If rats were used, they have a small body mass, so calculate how much essential oil they really used. Often the experiment used 5 ml of oil over five days. This is a highly irregular use of a concentrated essential oil.

See if they accounted for variables such as, type of oil, type of technique used, type of diluent etc.

Lastly did they come to logical conclusions? Were their findings "IF this --Then that" causal associations or were there correlations built on many repetitions of the same protocol?

Reading the Research:

Order of the Paper
    Abstract
    Introduction
    Methods
    Results
    Discussion

Order to read the Paper
    Abstract
    Discussion
    Introduction
    Results
    Methods

<u>What you should receive from the Abstract:</u>

1. Why - The purpose of the study. Why they performed the study.

2. How - The methodology summarizing the study design or How they performed the study.

3. What - Are the results of the study. What they found to be true based on design and data collected.

4. Meaning - The conclusion or the meaning they attached to the puzzle pieces collected is the study. What they say it means.

What is not in the abstract:

1. The puzzle pieces = white
   The puzzle pieces = orange
   The puzzle pieces = orange and white

2. Who - Look under the authors. Find out who they are and how they are funded and affiliated.

What you should receive from the Discussion:

1. Causation - How the results will support the conclusions.

2. Ask if you understand and believe the authors claims at this point.

3. Do these puzzle pieces fit together? Are puzzle pieces missing?

What you should receive from the Introduction:

1. This is the part where the research may or may not stimulate interest for what you were searching to use it for.
2. This area will relate the article to a larger context or point out relationships with other theories. Ask, does this substantiate what I believe? Ask, does this give me a new perspective on what I believe to be so?

3. The introduction should take you from something known to the specific area this study focused on. This is where we find the question they are trying to answer.

4. We are looking for Pugs. If you want cats, this is not your puzzle.

What you should receive from the Results:

1. This is the area of details of what they found, the data points or the puzzle pieces they collected.

2. This section should just contain what the data points are and not what they mean.

3. Look for any outliers and skewed data points here.

4. What are the puzzle pieces?

What you should receive from the Methods:

1. This is the study design. How and what was done.

2. This is often very technical language.

3. The research papers' purpose is to communicate with other researchers in the field, what was done and not to prove or validate anything.

4. How they came about collecting the puzzle pieces? 1 box? 6 boxes? Is there design bias?

When looking over the whole of the paper ask yourself:

1. What is the main point of this study?

2. Was it peer reviewed? Are these your peers?

3. What literature was reviewed?

4. What literature was cited to support their findings?

5. Are they qualified to interpret the data?

6. Are they using this research to skew meaning?

How do you find research studies?

1. The words you type in to find substantiated evidence of your claim will produce different results.

Quality of the input/question

=

Quality of the output/search results

2. What search engine you use will also change the outcome.

> Google
>
> vs
>
> Google Scholar
>
> vs
>
> Web of Science
>
> (Library of highly ranked papers – papers analyzed for significance)

3. There are many claims:
    a. Different types of Research Studies:

    Case Studies
    Clinical Studies
    Clinical Trials
    Double Blind Studies
    Meta-studies
    Incident reports
    Does the study fit my question?

    b. What is not a study?
    Testimonials.

    Unsubstantiated claims.

    Marketing language can be misdirecting and misleading.

4. Gain an understanding of the meaning of statistics:

Don't Freak Out ☺

Statistics are used to infer meaning and relationships. The more statistically significant the association between data points and causation the more the study substantiates the hypothesis or claim.

Hypothesis: All puzzle pieces are white.

Statistics: 98% of the time puzzle pieces are white.

TRUE For This Study Only!!

There are three core statistical concepts:

    A. Association vs Causation
    B. Correlation vs Multiple Regression
    C. Significance vs Magnitude

    A. <u>Association vs Causation</u>

    A&B tend to occur together more frequently than one would expect by random chance. Association does not prove causation.

Statistics only show associations that deviate from random chance NEVER causation

They infer or put meaning to causation from experimental design or theory combined with statistical associations that occur. In other words, statistics are used to support the theory. If you are looking for RED, you will see more RED, and therefore the stats will support your belief.

Hypothesis: Puzzle pieces are orange.
Statistics: 29% of puzzle pieces are orange in one study. 98% of puzzle pieces are orange in another study.
Both support hypothesis.
Here is an example of an A&B associated conclusion:

"It is noticed that sleeping in clothes and headaches occur together more than by chance."

Inference #1: A causes B
Going to sleep in your clothes causes headaches.

Inference #2: B causes A
Having a headache causes you to sleep in your clothes.

Inference #3: Some unaccounted variable caused A&B

Drinking causes you to sleep in your clothes and creates a headache.

B. <u>Correlation vs Multiple regression</u>

Correlation is recognizing that A&B tend to occur together more frequently than chance. A multiple regression tests the A&B correlation by comparing to things otherwise similar in certain ways.

For the above example compare this to ALL college students regardless of drinking and you will find drinking was the un-accounted for variable.

Here is another example:

Correlation:
    Pet owners, who believe their pets are family, visit vets more frequently.

Multiple regressions:
    Compare these "Pets are family" pet owners with similar pets or similar income brackets or similar –

areas of the country. This will account for more variables.

Pitbull vs Pug owners or 7-digit income or Beverly Hills vs Watts.

C. <u>Significance vs Magnitude</u>

These stats will tell how the small sample used in the research study would really or actually be evident in the general public.

Example: Testing a Bowl of Potato Soup.

Hypothesis: If there is potato in my sample then it is Potato Soup.

One sampling on a spoon yields NO POTATO.

Association – no potato in the spoon.

Correlation – Infers this is NOT potato soup.

Is the conclusion right?   Is it true?

Was the sample size poor?

Is it potato soup if your spoon does not contain a potato? When your spoon went in to get a sample is one sample enough?

Multiple Comparisons are needed to increase the Significance of the findings.

More data points change the results or outcome and validity of the study.

With our Puzzle example we found putting the whole puzzle together did not equal <u>all</u> pieces are white just by sampling enough pieces.

On with the Soup Example:

If you keep dipping the spoon into the soup – 30 times – the likelihood of finding a potato in the potato soup increases.

However, if you dip your spoon in beef soup and 1 out of 30 times you get a potato do you now have potato soup? No!

So sampling size increases the chances of improved data, but can also be used to skew data if need be.

The magnitude of the study increases its validity significantly. If you have one case study of using essential oils supporting musculoskeletal health, it is not statistically significant. (Testimonials)

However, if you have serial case studies showing effectiveness in 80 out of 100 cases, you now have a confidence interval of 80% using this essential oil blend increases musculoskeletal health.

Small numbers are often published when promoting or discounting essential oil use, and are not practically important as conclusions.

Returning to our soup example:

You use 100 spoons in the soup, and 95 spoons have potato on them. You now have a 95% confidence interval that the soup is potato soup.

> *Any product claim must be truthful, not misleading and substantiated with enough data*

Use the right research to substantiate and support your findings. Case studies may or may not be valid research depending on whom you talk to. Serial Case Studies have a higher confidence level.

> **Substantial evidence to me is all about consistency of results and numbers**

Example: Water helps dehydration. How do we know this? Many, many, many case studies. Out of data points emerge patterns to consider. These patterns then lead to designed studies.

A product claim is NOT evidence. Do not do a Google search and think you are finding substantiated valid research claims. Searches are more and more untrue. There are books on qualitative inquiry or grounded theory research.

This research model suggests that you collect data and then let the data reveal a pattern, which in turn will stimulate further testing of the pattern, revealed.[7]

Example:

I used a blend in my practice 250 times.

I collected data of effectiveness and any side effects.

I organized those data points and made correlations between them.

I concluded that the blend was highly efficient at relieving musculoskeletal pain with very low incidence of side effects.

I then tested 250 more pets to see if my conclusion (hypothesis), or how I put the puzzle pieces together, was, in fact, true.

> **After 500 case studies – I felt confident that this blend is a good choice to use in pets**

If it is published, does that make it true?
If it is on the Internet, does that make it true?
If it is in a book, does that make it true?
What is substantiation?

The full definition of SUBSTANTIATE[8] is:

> 1: To give substance or form to : embody
> 2: To establish by proof or competent evidence : verify
> <substantiate a charge>

Data and observation, without bias, will give form to or embody the truth. Serial Case studies are competent evidence to verify claims.

MUCH RESEARCH IS INVALID AND FLAWED TODAY

We have established observation is flawed by:
Expected outcome = RED vs GREEN.

Right vs Truth = Number of puzzle pieces □ △ ◊
and unknown/unaccounted for variables = apples to oranges.

I can find a scientific study to support my belief of what happens every time. I can find a study to support and to debunk my findings every time. Is Research really the only evidence of safe and effective? Is Research really the only evidence of dangerous? Is Research right or true? Depends on the rigor of the Researcher.

To Quote Research by Researchers from "Verification Strategies for Establishing Reliability and Validity in Qualitative Research":

"The quality of controlled trials is of obvious relevance to systematic reviews. If the 'raw material' is flawed, then the conclusions of systematic reviews cannot be trusted by meta-studies. Many reviewers formally assess the quality of primary trials by following the recommendations of the Cochrane Collaboration and other experts."

A Method to use to Judge Validity:

The methodology for both the assessment of quality and its incorporation into systematic reviews and meta-analysis are a matter of ongoing debate. In this article we discuss the concept of study quality and the methods used to assess quality of the components of internal and external validity of controlled clinical trials.

- *Internal validity*—extent to which systematic error (bias) is minimized in clinical trials
- *Selection bias:* biased allocation to comparison groups
- *Performance bias:* unequal provision of care apart from treatment under evaluation
- *Detection bias:* biased assessment of outcome
- *Attrition bias:* biased occurrence and handling of deviations from protocol and loss to follow up
- *External validity*—extent to which results of trials provide a correct basis for generalization to other circumstances
- *Patients:* age, sex, severity of disease and risk factors, co-morbidity
- *Treatment regimens:* dosage, timing and route of administration, type of treatment within a class of treatments, concomitant treatments
- *Settings:* level of care (primary to tertiary) and experience and specialization of care provider
- *Modalities of outcomes:* type or definition of outcomes and duration of follow up
- *Quality is a multidimensional concept, which could relate to the design, conduct, and analysis of a trial, its clinical relevance, or quality of reporting*

> **The validity of the findings generated by a study clearly is an important dimension of quality, substantiation and value of the study**

"The rejection of reliability and validity in qualitative inquiry in the 1980s has resulted in an interesting <u>shift for "ensuring rigor"</u> from the investigator's actions during the course of the research, <u>to the reader or consumer</u> of the qualitative inquiry…"

We the reader should ascertain if the study is valid? REALLY!

"The emphasis on strategies that are implemented during the research process has been replaced by strategies for evaluating trustworthiness and utility that are implemented <u>once a study is completed</u>. In this article, we argue that reliability and validity remain appropriate concepts for attaining rigor in qualitative research."

Validity of the study is judged after not before and during.

"We argue that qualitative researchers should reclaim responsibility for reliability and validity by implementing verification strategies integral and self-correcting during the conduct of inquiry itself.[9]"

Research should have stringent quality control rules.

"This ensures the attainment of rigor using strategies inherent within each qualitative design, and <u>moves the responsibility</u> for incorporating and maintaining reliability and validity <u>from external reviewers' judgments to the investigators themselves.</u>"

Investigators should be held to standards of validity.

"*Finally, we make a plea for a return to terminology for ensuring rigor that is used by mainstream science[10].*"

Let's all get on the same page.

> **In common language, this is a researcher who researches research saying that research is not held to a standard of validity**

Evidence Based Medicine

The definition of evidence-based practice, according to Sackett[11] and colleagues is:

"*conscientious, explicit, and judicious use of current best evidence in making decisions about the care of individual patients.*"

Straus and colleagues also described it as the:

"*integration of best research evidence with our clinical expertise and our patient's unique values and circumstances.*"

These statements mean that evidence informs practice, but should not dictate it.

It is vital that all health care practitioners keep each patient's unique factors in mind when deciding if research findings should be applied, modified, or completely rejected.

It is the clinical decision making that is critical!

Argument for Case Studies as Evidence Based Medicine

"The Kuhnian insight, concludes, that a scientific discipline without a large number of thoroughly executed case studies is a discipline without systematic production of exemplars, and a discipline without exemplars is <u>an ineffective one</u>.[12]"

Please note there are differences between case studies and testimonials. A Testimonial is used in a court of law to provide evidence. A Case study is used in the medical field to supply the need for further inquiry. Here is yet another double standard. A person could go to prison based on the eyewitness testimonial of one person, yet the medical industry will not use 500 case studies as valid. Evidence-Based-Medicine.

The American Holistic Veterinary Medical Foundation (AHVMF) is a nonprofit organization that funds investigations to advance animal health through integrative holistic veterinary medicine. The AHVMF is a 501(c)(3) nonprofit organization. Tax ID: 26-1583307. Please donate to www.ahvmf.org

Full Definition of TESTIMONIAL[13]

1:   Evidence, testimony
2a : A statement testifying to benefits received
2b : A character reference: letter of recommendation
3:   An expression of appreciation: tribute

Definition of CASE STUDY[14]

1: An intensive analysis of an individual unit (as a person or community) stressing developmental factors in relation to environment

> In short, the veterinarians using essential oils in the field are your current best resource for safe and effective use of Veterinary Medical Aromatherapy® VMAA.vet .

PART V: cGMP/QC - PICKING PARTNERS

As a professor of pharmacology and pharmacognosy at a medical school, I teach about cGMP/QC. We discuss the importance of the steps to take when purchasing products to use in medical practice. You would want to know that the products you choose online, at a health food store or in a drug store, are both safe and effective, correct? Many of us just assume that what we buy is safe and effective. This is not necessarily true.

FDA is not authorized to review dietary supplement products for safety and effectiveness before they are marketed[15]

"Manufacturers are required to produce dietary supplements in a quality manner and ensure that they do not contain contaminants or impurities, and are accurately labeled according to current Good Manufacturing Practice (cGMP) and labeling regulations[16]."

cGMP is "current Good Manufacturing Practices". These are the standards followed in every step of the process to develop the product you are choosing to promote or use; from the raw materials to the containers used. Standards of production should be rigidly adhered to every step of the way. Outstanding cGMP increases outstanding products and ncreases outstanding wellness.

Questions to ask in regards to Biologically Active® essential oil current Good Manufacturing Practices:

Ask yourself at the time of purchase and educate your Nose:

1. Are fragrances subtle, rich, organic, and delicate?

2. Do they "feel" natural?

3. Do the fragrances vary from batch to batch?

Questions to ask the retailer:

1. Is each batch tested with 10 different analysis?

2. Do independent labs test them?

3. Does the supplier grow and distill their own organically grown plants?

4. Are the oils distilled in-house, fresh and by rigid standards of distillation?

5. Does their supplier use low pressure and low temperature to distill essential oils and preserve all of their fragile chemical constituents?

6. Are the distillation cookers made from stainless steel to reduce chemically reacting with metal?

7. Does the supplier inspect the fields and distillers worldwide from whom they buy?

8. Are they checking each step of the way that no synthetic chemicals are being used in any of the processes?

9. Are the oils being produced for commercial use or are they produced by higher standards to result in a Biologically Active® essential oil?

10. Is the goal profit (biggest yield of oil) or Quality (capturing the full essence of what the plant has to offer?.

11. What is the focus of the company leaders and what is their integrity?

12. Does the company offer a guarantee of quality?

The following are questions were developed by Dr. David Stewart[17] and modified by me to have a starting point to access cGMP for essential oil producers and retailers:

1. Does their company own any farms on which to raise plants for essential oils? And if they do, are they new farms on land formerly polluted with herbicides, pesticides, and chemicals that contain residuals from the past, or are they farming land that is clean, which has never been cultivated or been un-tilled for at least the last 50 years?

2. Does their company have their own fully equipped testing laboratory to verify an oil's composition? Do they invest in equipment that can detect adulterant and synthetic essential oils? Can they differentiate between natural and adulteration? Do they contract with partner farms under stringent cGMP.

3. Do they have anyone on staff with a trained nose who can analyze oils by their smell? Have you learned to train your Nose?

4. If their company purchases oils from outside suppliers, do they visit the distilleries and farms of those suppliers periodically to observe if the herbs are grown organically- without pesticides, herbicides, or chemical fertilizers? What standards do they require these partner farms to adhere to?

5. Do they know if the grower has a testing laboratory on the farm to determine when the crop is at its peak for oil harvesting? Is the company's first priority to quality or to quantity? Is this company transparent and integridous?

6. Do they know if the crops were actually harvested at their peak time and, if so, were there an inordinate delay in taking them to the still and into the cookers? What are the standards they are using to produce Biologically Active® essential oils?

7. Do they know if their distillery personnel understand the art and science of distilling? Exactly how to pack the cookers, how to administer the steam, how to maintain minimum temperatures and pressures throughout the cooker? How to continuously monitor the process throughout distillation to make sure the oil produced contains all of its components in the proper proportions?

In other words are they a company that produces oils or are they a company that sells oils? Remember focus is everything.

8. If their supplier makes a mistake in the distillation harvesting processes that results in an inferior grade of oil, does that supplier sell the oil anyway or do they discard it?

9. Do they know if the cookers in the distilleries of their suppliers have domed lids or cone shaped lids? Has this company developed the highest standards of production in the industry of essential oils?

10. Do they know if their suppliers supplement the distillation process with solvents to extract additional oil from the plant matter? Sometimes these practices yield more oil but are of inferior quality and it will take special testing equipment to detect these practices. Does this company test for these practices?

11. Do they know if their suppliers bottle their oils directly from the distillery without modifying the composition of the natural oil by adding anything or taking anything away? In what part of production are they performing quality control testing procedures? They should test at the start, in the middle and at the end to ensure what is in the bottle is

what we expect in a Biologically Active® essential oil. Is it a common practice to dilute the essential oils, single or blends, and market them as 100% pure essential oils? Do they dilute the oils? If they do, how do we know how much essential oil to use therapeutically?

For instance, if a protocol calls for 15 drops of an undiluted product how many drops would you need to use of theirs? A cost difference may be evident in the conversion.

12. Do they know if their company has tested their company's oils side by side with the Gold Standard in the industry in the same lab to make a fair comparison? And if so, where is the data? If they claim to be "better" where is the proof?

This is not a complete comprehensive list of questions you could ask, but if their answer to any or most of the above is "no," or "I don't know," then how do they know their oils are "Biologically Active® essential oils"? Without such knowledge, how can they make any verifiable claims?

QC equals Quality Control. These are the methods used to test the product once it has been manufactured. These tests should be verified against stringent standards.

Questions to ask in regards to Biologically Active® essential oil Quality Control:

1. Does testing begin upon receiving oil at the distiller even before it leaves the distiller?
2. Is the testing in-house <u>and</u> 3rd party (independent) testing?

3. Where in manufacturing is testing done? The minimum is three testing points along the way, at the start, in the middle, and at the end in the bottle.

4. Is Quality Control testing done in-house <u>and</u> 3rd party <u>with</u> comprehensive <u>up-to-date</u> equipment?

5. Is there a division of the company where analysis can be done when testing reveals a problem and then corrective steps can be made?

The company you order oils from should do <u>all</u> of the following testing:

1. cGMP should include measurable standards and quality control regulated in house with stringent standards. The standards and findings should be transparent to the consumer.
2. GCMS - Gas Chromatography Mass Spectrometry.

Lists every chemical compound by identification. This test is not specific to where the chemical came from the plant, distilling practice or adulteration.

3. IRMS - Isotope Ratio Mass Spectrometry.
   This machine will test for naturally occurring isotopes.

   The ratio of isotopes, carbon 12-13-14, that plants take in from CO_2 is a fixed ratio of carbon isotopes.
   If the oil is synthetic (made in a lab) or adulterated, they will not have the same ratio. This testing tells natural from synthetic.

4. FTIR - Fortier Transform Infrared Spectroscopy.
   This equipment measures bonds between the compounds and how they interact. Essential oils are a synergy between compounds, not a sum of their parts (chemical constituents).

5. Quick tests – these tests are done to eliminate many batches of oils that do not adhere to stringent standards before they ever reach the more comprehensive tests.

a. Specific gravity - The thickness of the oil.
b. Refractive index - How much the oil bends light.
c. Denstritometry - How much water is in the oil.
d. Polarimetery - Rotation of the chemicals.

Each essential oil has strict guidelines. For instance, if there is a lot of water in the oil, then the distillation process was done at substandard.

6. ICP - Inductively Coupled Plasma Optical Emission Spectrometry.
   This instrument picks up the Parts Per Billion (ppB) range of metals. Testing for heavy metal contamination.

7. CC - Chiral Chromatography.
   This equipment will separate optical isomers, the mirror images of the same molecule. Natural unadulterated essential oils are put together differently from synthetic poor quality oils. Molecules can have a different 3-dimensional orientation like our hands, right and left, are mirror images. Synthesized essential oils will be a racemic mixture, equal ratios of right and left spinning or oriented molecules of the same chemical. Nature will have <u>ONLY ONE</u> optical isomer that it creates. This is a test that tells natural from synthetic.

Kurt Schnaubelt PhD., my mentor, is a world renowned chemist in the study of essential oils. He said to me in a private conversation that the industry of essential oils is big money and therefore, the profiteers are looking for ways to trick the testing equipment.

He stated the only thing they have not yet learned to duplicate in the lab from nature, is the ratio of the optical isomers. We must be ever vigilant in our quest to recognize natural from synthesized and adulterated essential oils. He states this, also, in his most current book, "Healing Intelligence of Essential Oils"[18].

Kurt goes on to say that the essential oils co-evolved with us, from the primordial soup and therefore ONLY the natural or Biologically Active® product will produce healing effects on biological systems such as pets and humans.[19]

What is in that bottle of essential oils does matter! They are not all created equal by any means. I have conducted hundreds of tests for safety and efficacy and can tell you very few can measure up to these standards. Most oils have caused side effects due to poor cGMP and QC. Many studies have no idea to select for these variables and have thus reported data findings on the essential oil and created a causal association that their findings are applicable to ALL essential oils. They are WRONG.
Most consumers conclude there is no difference - They are VERY wrong.

It is time the industry digs deep into their methodology and up their standards of research.

Conclusion:

Start applying these techniques by doing a Google search or a FaceBook search for a news broadcast, article or paper about an area of interest like aromatherapy for pets. Make a copy of what you read and print it out. See if it can stand up to the Dig Deep method.

Start using precision language and get curious about what others think. Be genuinely interested in the way they came to a conclusion. I may go research it more and even find that there were some pearls of wisdom in their belief too.

The quickest way to build a relationship is to align with their perspective and walk in their shoes. If they are a true friend, they will be willing to do the same with you.

Lastly, please get, as a consumer, not all essential oils are safe and effective. Choose to Dig Deep!
Please go to www.safe4animals.com for further information on applying these methods.

On VMAA.vet there is a video on the Dig Deep method.

Thank you so much again for spending your time and energy with me, Dr. Nancy Brandt, digging deep into your own belief systems thus finding new treasures.

There are over 600,000 plants and only 5% are thoroughly investigated and recognized for aromatic and medicinal advantages

Yes I have the research to support this statement

*The Earth is the Garden of Eden
We have only lost the knowledge of it
We are now rediscovering what the animal
and plant kingdom already knows
We must reconnect*

Bibliography:

Editor: Anna Doell, CAA

Editor: Linda Phillips, Reiki Master, CAC

Photos courtesy of Jermaine Freeman

Resources:

Mining foreman R. Thornburg shows a small cage with a canary used for testing carbon monoxide gas in 1928. (George McCaa, U.S. Bureau of Mines)

www.xpar.org

blogdiStefaniaDemetz

DOG-DIGGING-SAND
By Sue Wills | Published 30/10/2015

Cate Frost
Royalty-free stock photo ID: 736484
Woman finds needle in a haystack
Quick Shot
Royalty-free stock photo ID: 540585358
Billion Photos
Royalty-free stock photo ID: 259913525
Scales of Justice, Weight Scale, Balance.
Magdalena Kucova
Royalty-free stock photo ID: 144403597
Detail of bowl with potato soup and wooden ladle
Rob Hyrons
Royalty-free stock photo ID: 179665787
a man banging his head against the wall in frustration
Linda Bucklin
Royalty-free stock illustration ID: 12400552
3D render of a giant fly holding a blank sign.
Valentina Razumova
Royalty-free stock photo ID: 128628794

ocean_fo
Royalty-free stock illustration ID: 489720835
Human brain illustrated with interconnected small nerves
 Dwight Smith
Royalty-free stock photo ID: 3805840
An orphaned kitten in a cage reaching out with a paw
vvvita
Royalty-free stock photo ID: 655149775
Happy little girl walking with dog on the field
John T Takai
Royalty-free stock vector ID: 33985009
grieving man
Eric Isselee
Royalty-free stock photo ID: 299129312
Group of parrots in front of a white background
Stock_VectorSale
Royalty-free stock vector ID: 618537242
OLEH SLEPCHENKO
Royalty-free stock photo ID: 701370541
Environmental pollution. Plastic bottles, bags, trash in river or lake. Rubbish and pollution floating in water.
Subbotina Anna
Royalty-free stock photo ID: 131008628
Lavender
Sonsedska Yuliia
Royalty-free stock photo ID: 553685038
Beautiful cat Scottish Straight, lying on his back, isolated on white background
Shavlovskiy
Royalty-free stock photo ID: 483263275
Pieces of a puzzle
Nikiforov Volodymyr
Royalty-free stock photo ID: 131750936
Hands placing last piece of a Puzzle
maradon 333
Royalty-free stock photo ID: 576831568
two hands trying to connect couple puzzle piece with sunset background.
Osetrik
Royalty-free stock photo ID: 523227928

Beautiful bay horse.
 Nicole Ciscato
Royalty-free stock photo ID: 249053572
Clydesdale with driving tack details
noraneko design
Royalty-free stock vector ID: 565436062
Male office worker thinks
matrioshka
Royalty-free stock vector ID: 566491378
Old pirate treasure map.
Ermolaev Alexander
Royalty-free stock photo ID: 485954863
Smart dog and funny cat reading a book.
Iryna Kuznetsova
Royalty-free stock photo ID: 766626844
The cat teacher wrote on a blackboard "All dogs are stupid"
Annette Shaff
Royalty-free stock photo ID: 178333340
a dog peeking into a dirt hole in the ground
hurricanehank
Royalty-free stock photo ID: 421322464
Little Jack Russell puppy playing on beach digging sand.
Royalty-free stock photo ID: 211047988
Cute dog works in the office at the computer. Concentration and strictly looking at the screen
fizkes
Royalty-free stock photo ID: 1075401590
Grateful boss

Footnotes:

1. Carl Allman, private conversation, 2018

2. Revista Brasileira de Farmacognosia Behavioral effects of essential oil of *Citrus aurantium* L. inhalation in rats www.scielo.br/scielo.php?script=sci_arttext&pid=S0102-695X2008000500003.

3. www.safe4animals.com

4. "Essential Oils Safety" Second Edition Robert Tisserand and Rodney Young, 2013, Page 1

5. "Unlimited Possibilities" Proceedings of the 8th International Aromatherapy Conference, Kurt Schnaubelt, Editor, 2015, Page 97

6. "Leadership Academy", Robbins Research International, Inc., Tony Robbins, 2006, Page 182

7. Strategies of Qualitative Inquiry, Norman K. Denzin, Yvonne S. Lincoln, 2013

8. www.merriam-webster.com/dictionary/substantiate

9. Strategies of Qualitative Inquiry, Norman K. Denzin, Yvonne S. Lincoln, 2013

10. Verification Strategies for Establishing Reliability and Validity in Qualitative Research, Janice M. Morse, Michael Barrett, Maria Mayan, Karin Olson, Jude Spiers Abstract

11. David Sackett and the birth of Evidence *Based Medicine: How to Practice and Teach EBM 4e BMJ* 2015; 350

12. Five Misunderstandings About Case-Study Research, Bent Flyvbjerg, Qualitative Inquiry, vol 12, no. 2, April 2006, Pages 219-245

13. www.merriam-webster.com/dictionary/testimonial

14. www.merriam-webster.com/dictionary/case%20study

15. www.fda.gov/food/dietarysupplements/usingdietarysupplements

16. www.fda.gov/Food/DietarySupplements/UsingDietarySupplements/ucm109760.htm

17. Chemistry of Essential Oils Made Simple, Dr. David Stewart, Ph.D, 2013

18. The Healing Intelligence of Essential Oils: The Science of Advance Aromatherapy, Dr. Kurt Schnaubelt, Ph.D, D.M.N., 2011

19. Dr. Kurt Schnaubelt, Ph.D, M.N.M, first VMAA Conference Keynote Speaker, 2018